ISBN- 13: 978-1544133218
ISBN-10: 1544133219

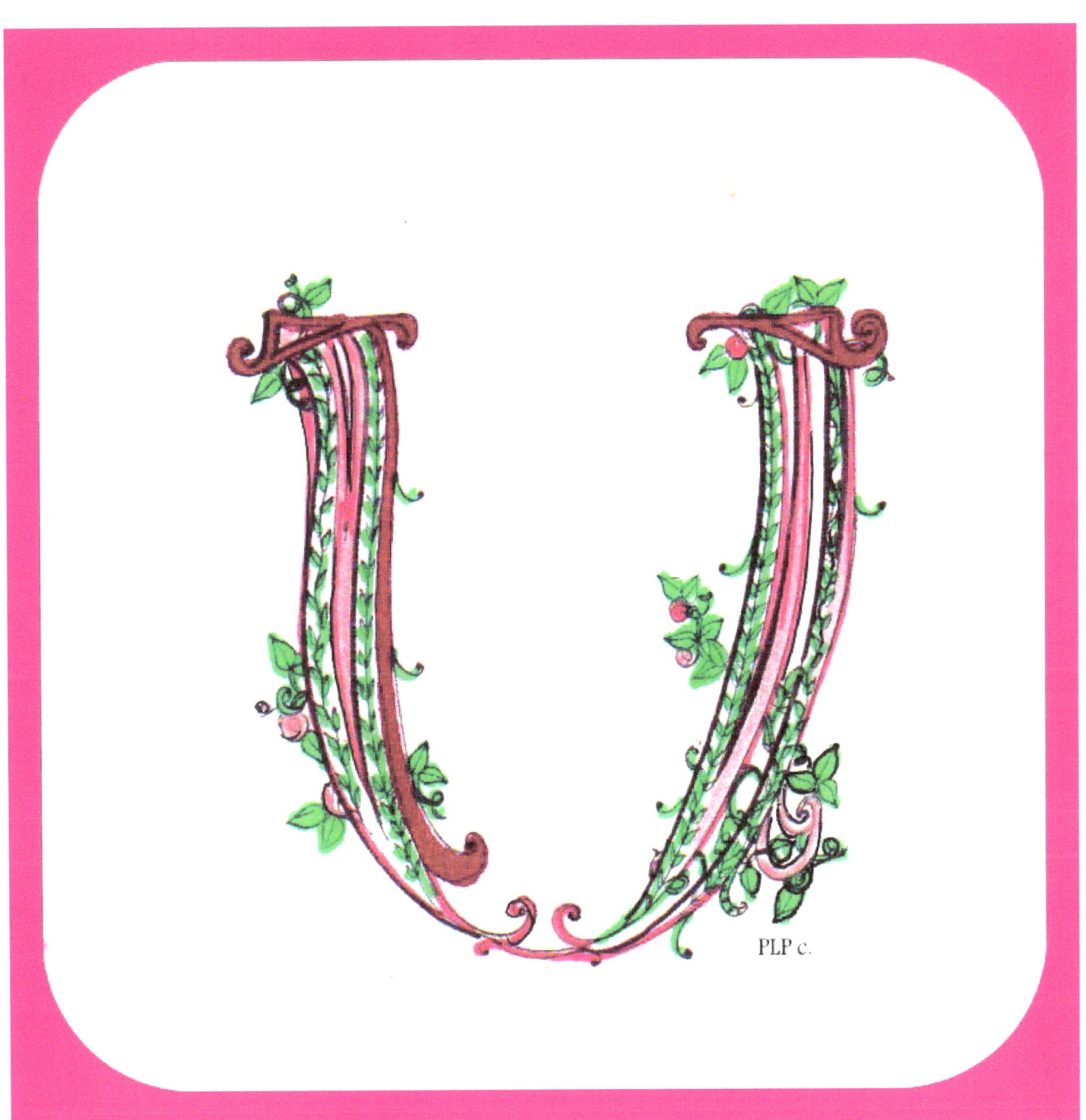

PLP c.

The Unique Letter U

Coloring Book

By Peggy Louise Parrish
c. 2017

The Unique U is very fun to color

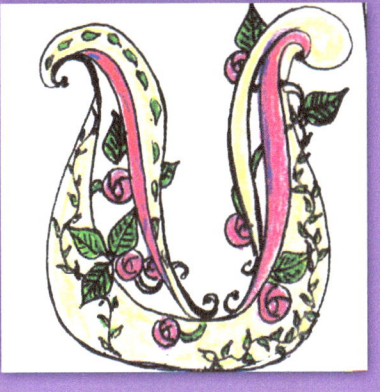 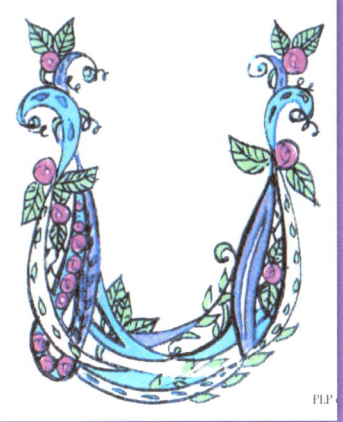 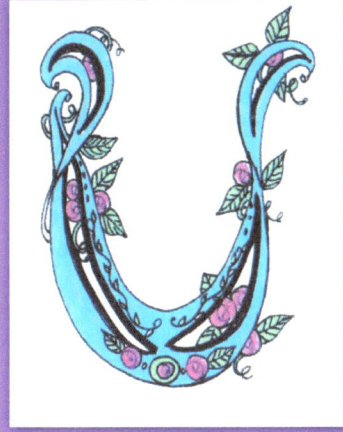

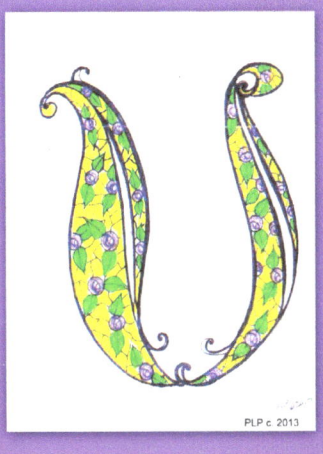 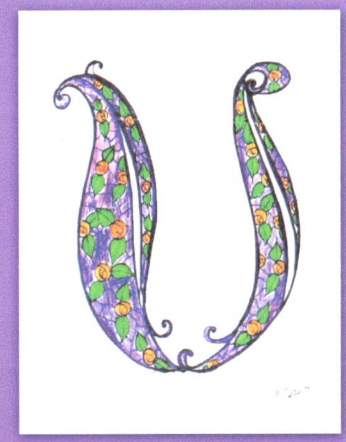 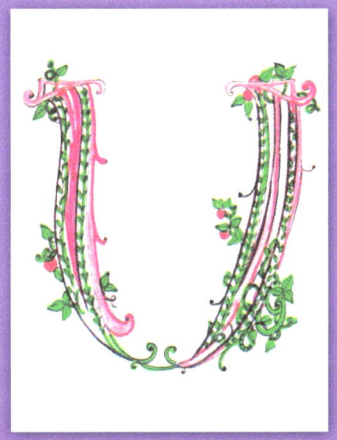

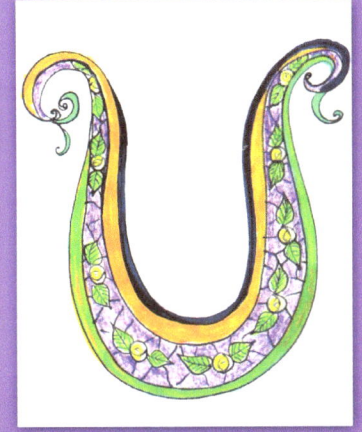 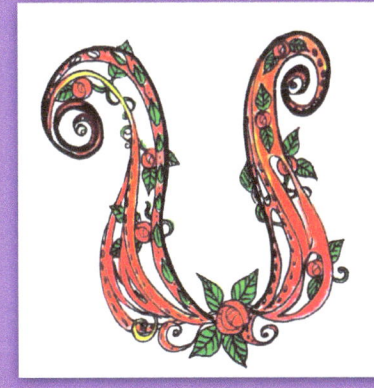 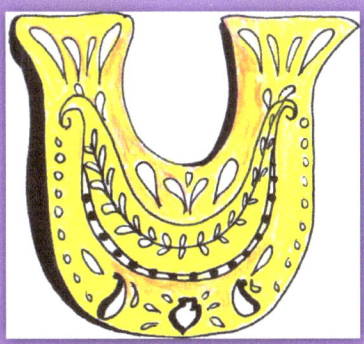

Which one is your favorite?

Welcome to the UNIQUE U

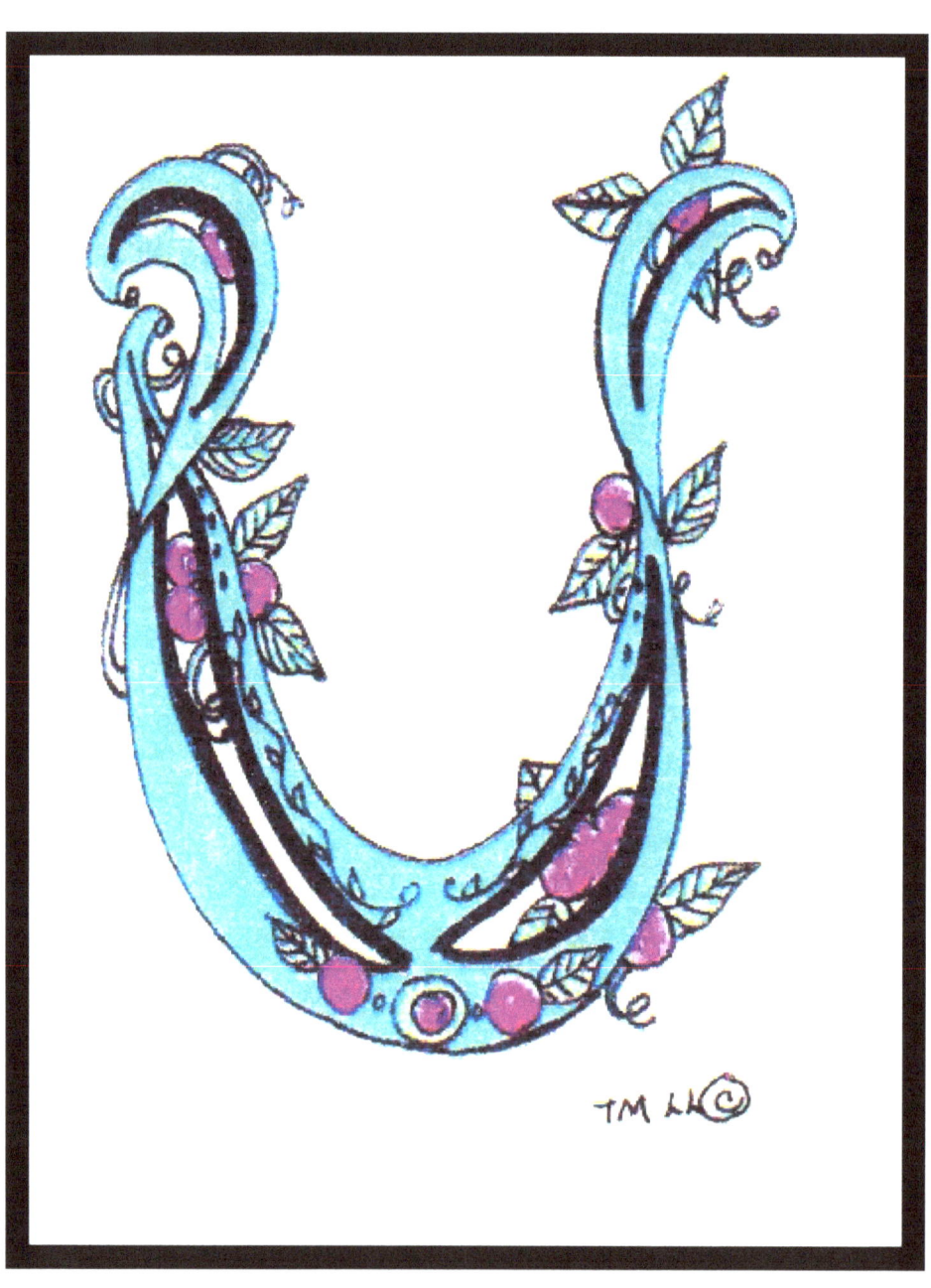

Welcome to an adventure with the Unique Letter U. There will be over 20 designs of Letter U for you to color. Quality colored pencils are the preferred medium used with these letter pages. If you want to use markers, gel pens, watercolor pencils or paints you need to place a scrap paper behind the pages as you color. If you leave the initials of the artist PLP on the bottom of the letter design you may make a few "in house' copies to color several different ways.

Perhaps your first or last name begins with a letter U. If so you will probably find a lot of fun in the next pages . You may want to use one of these U letters to start a name or word after you have colored it.

If you enjoy this book take a look at the other letter books by artist Peggy Louise Parrish . May you enjoy visiting these U pages with your coloring.

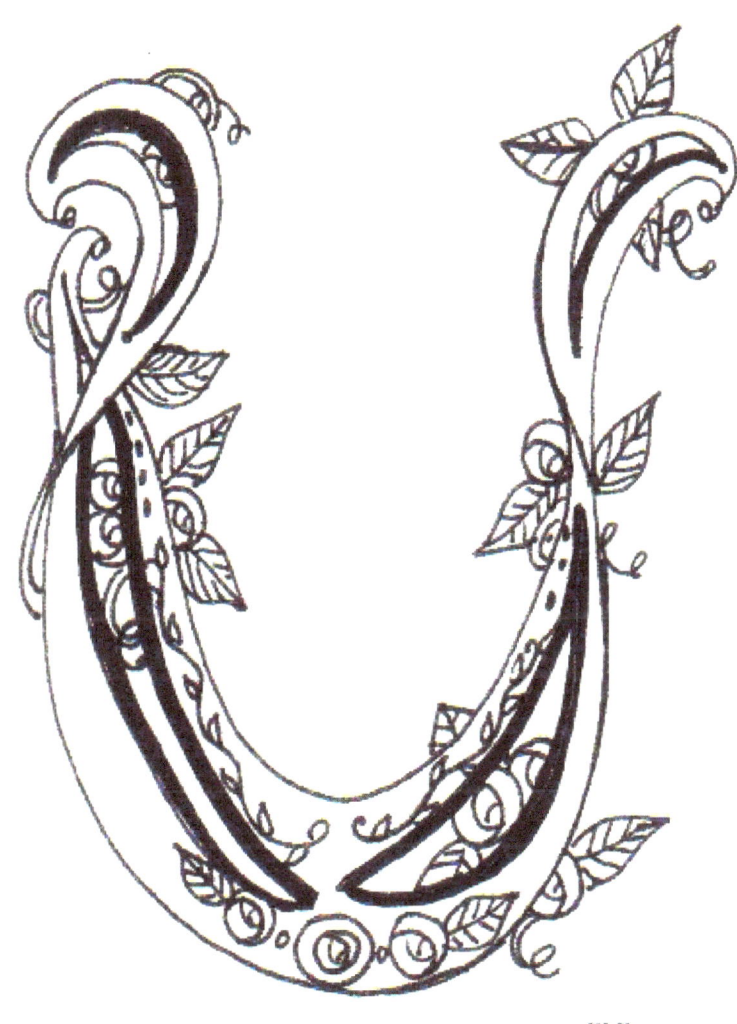

PLP c.

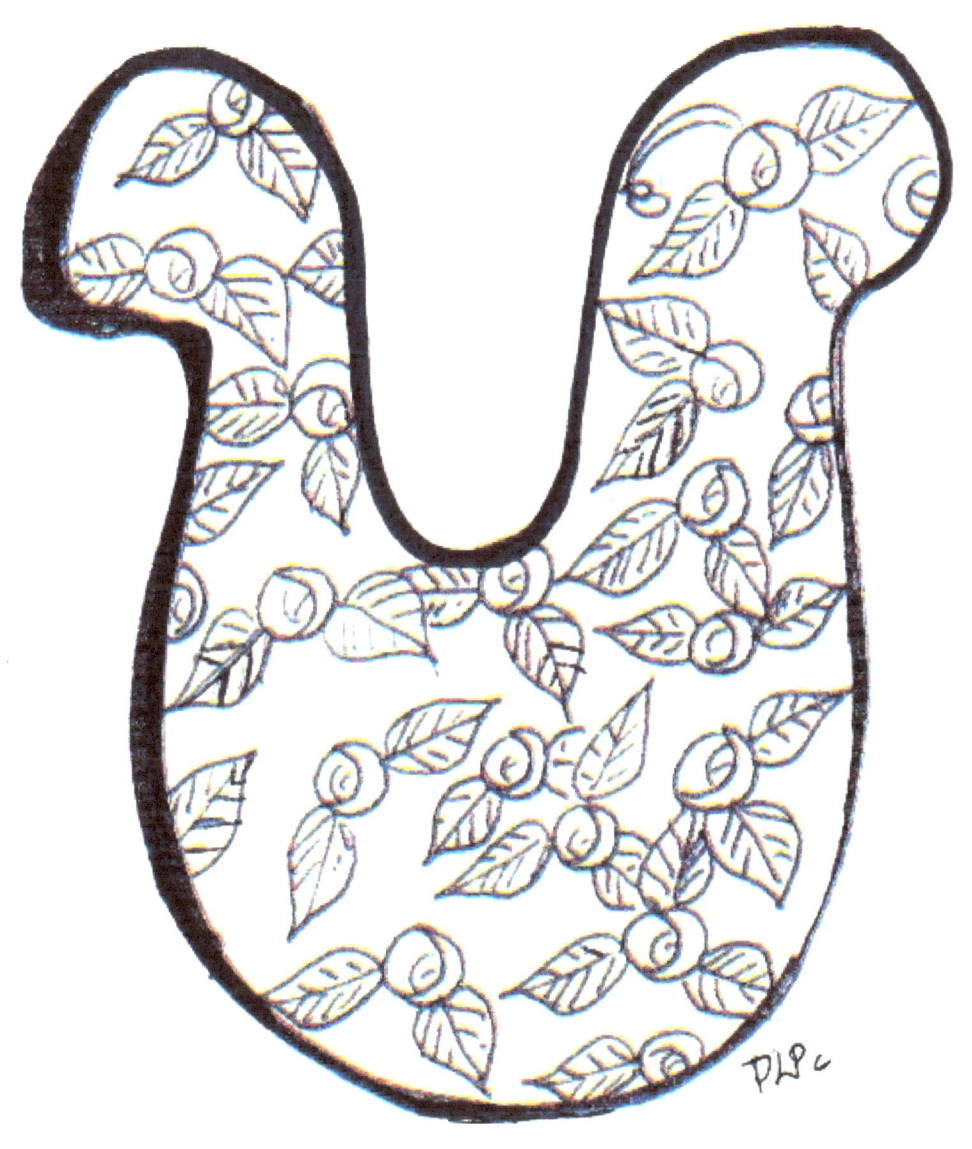

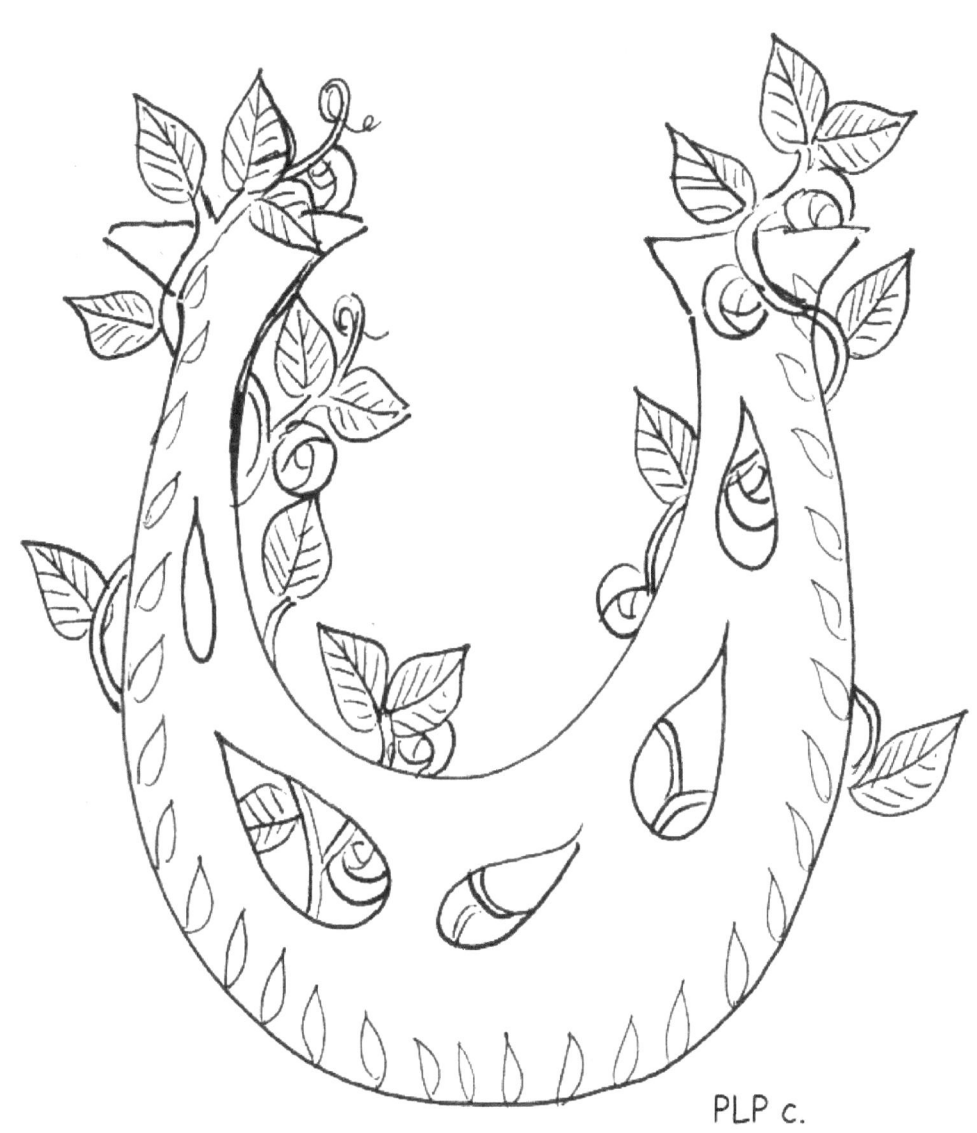

PLP c.

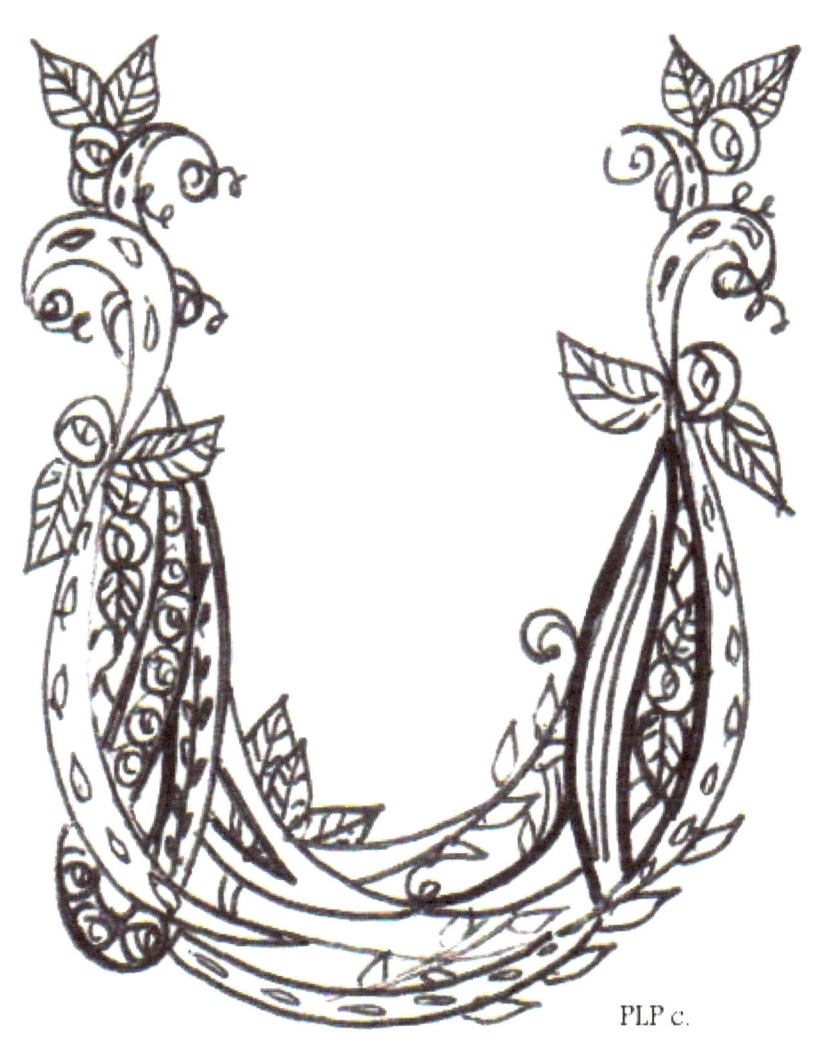

PLP c.

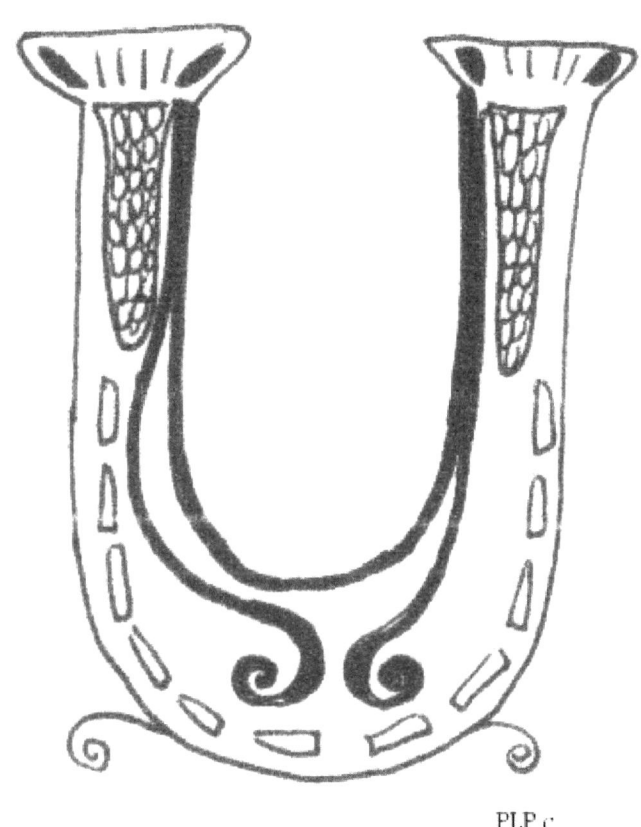

PLP c.

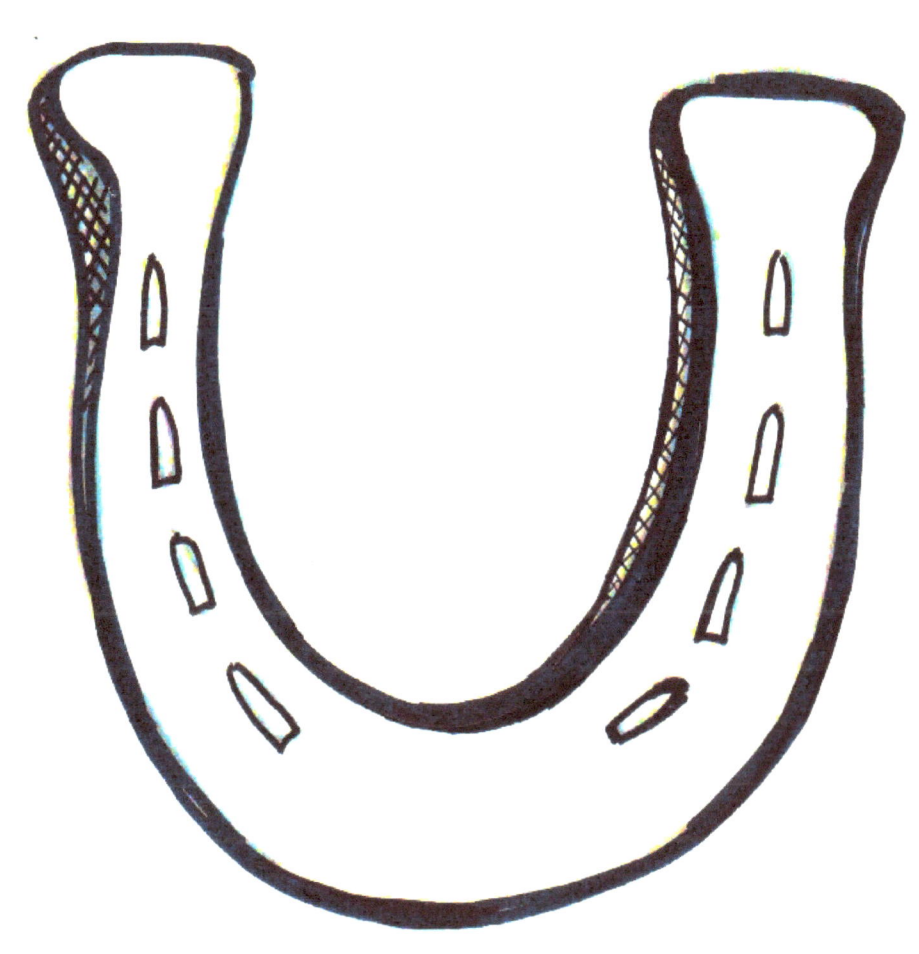

PLP c.

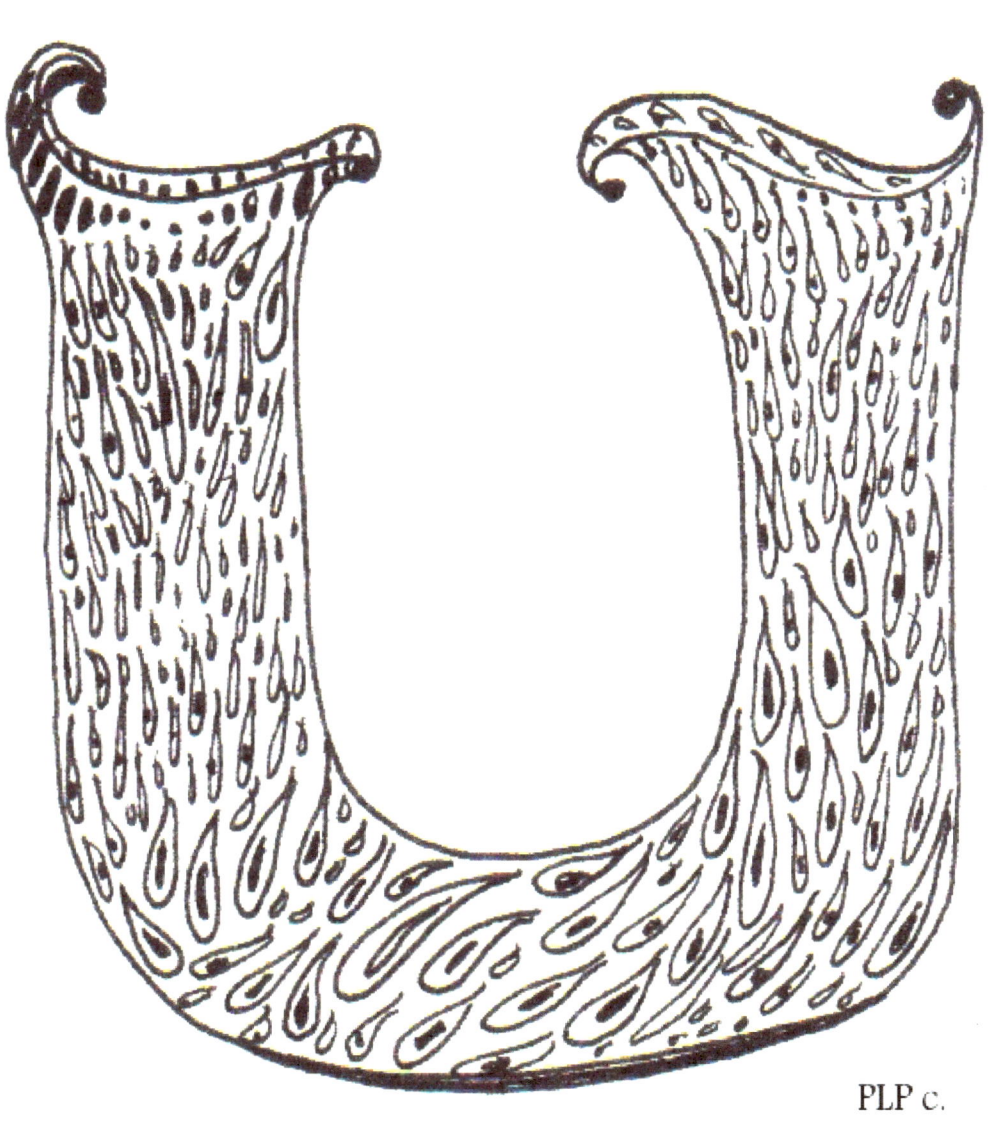

PLP c.

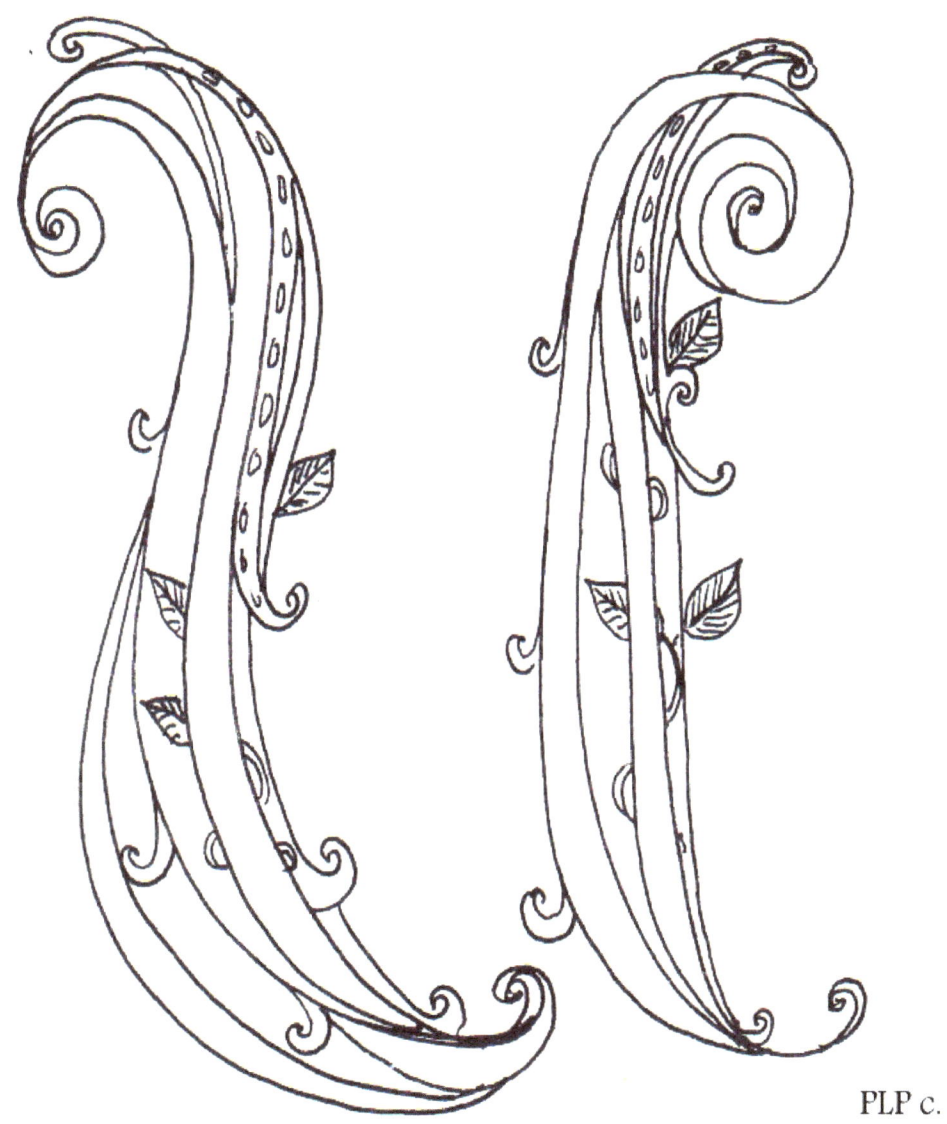

PLP c.

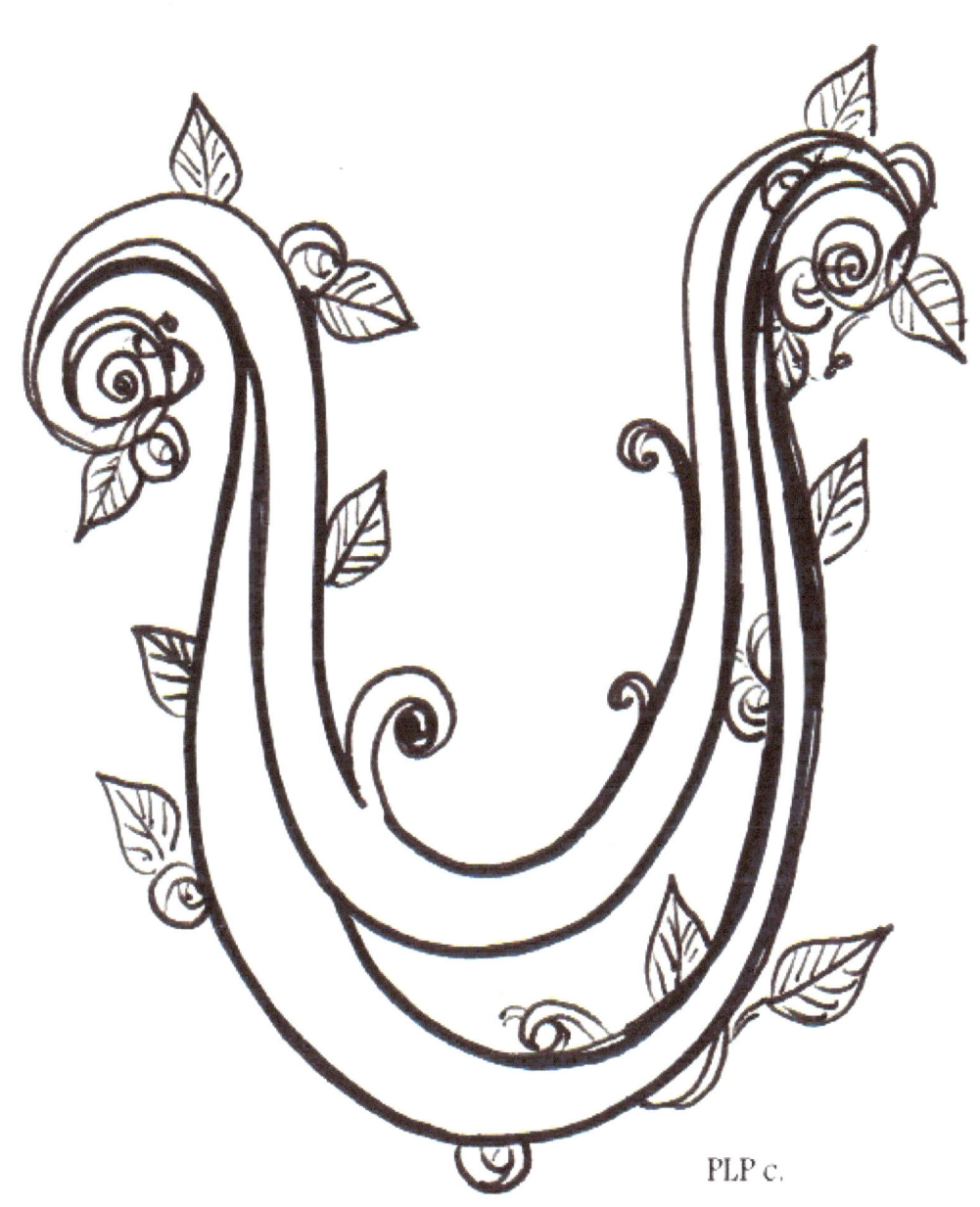

PLP c.

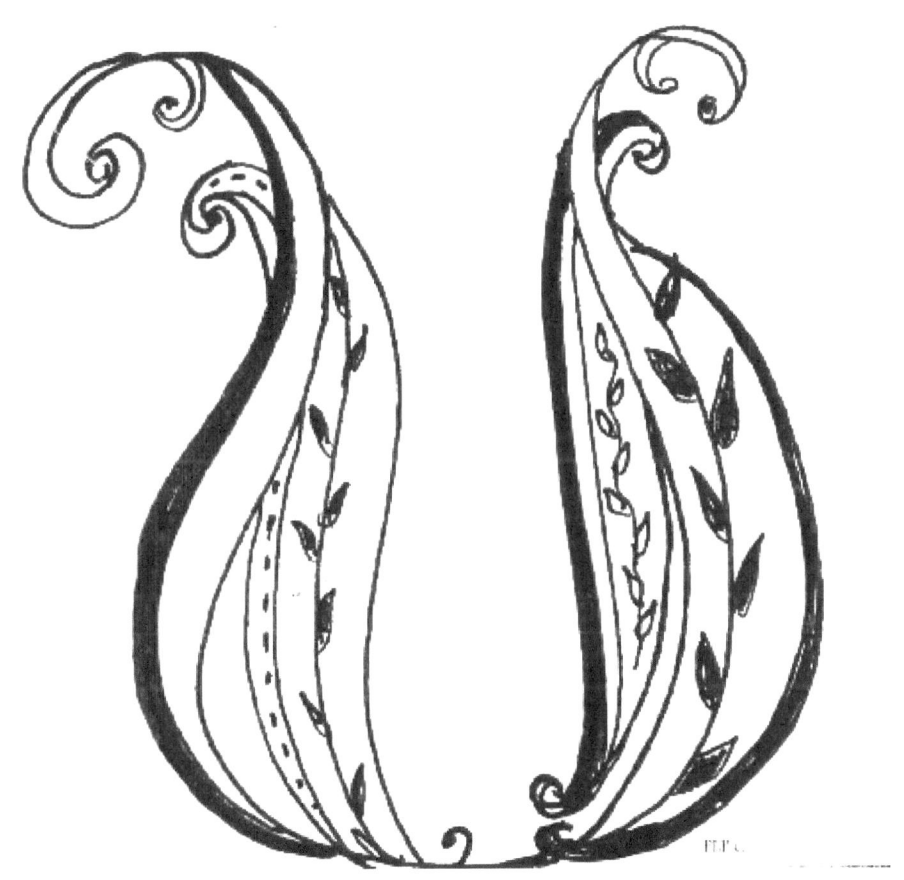

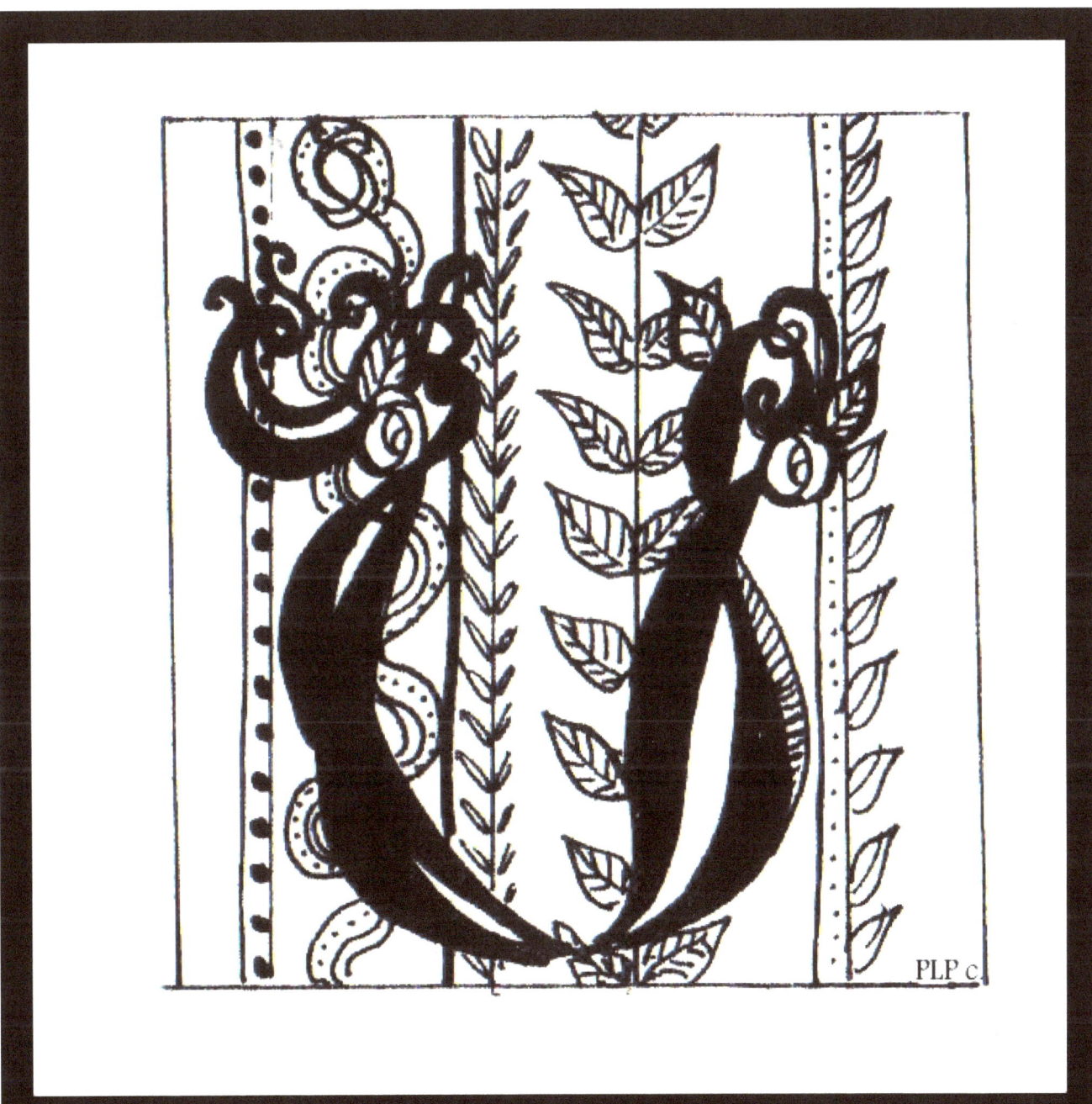

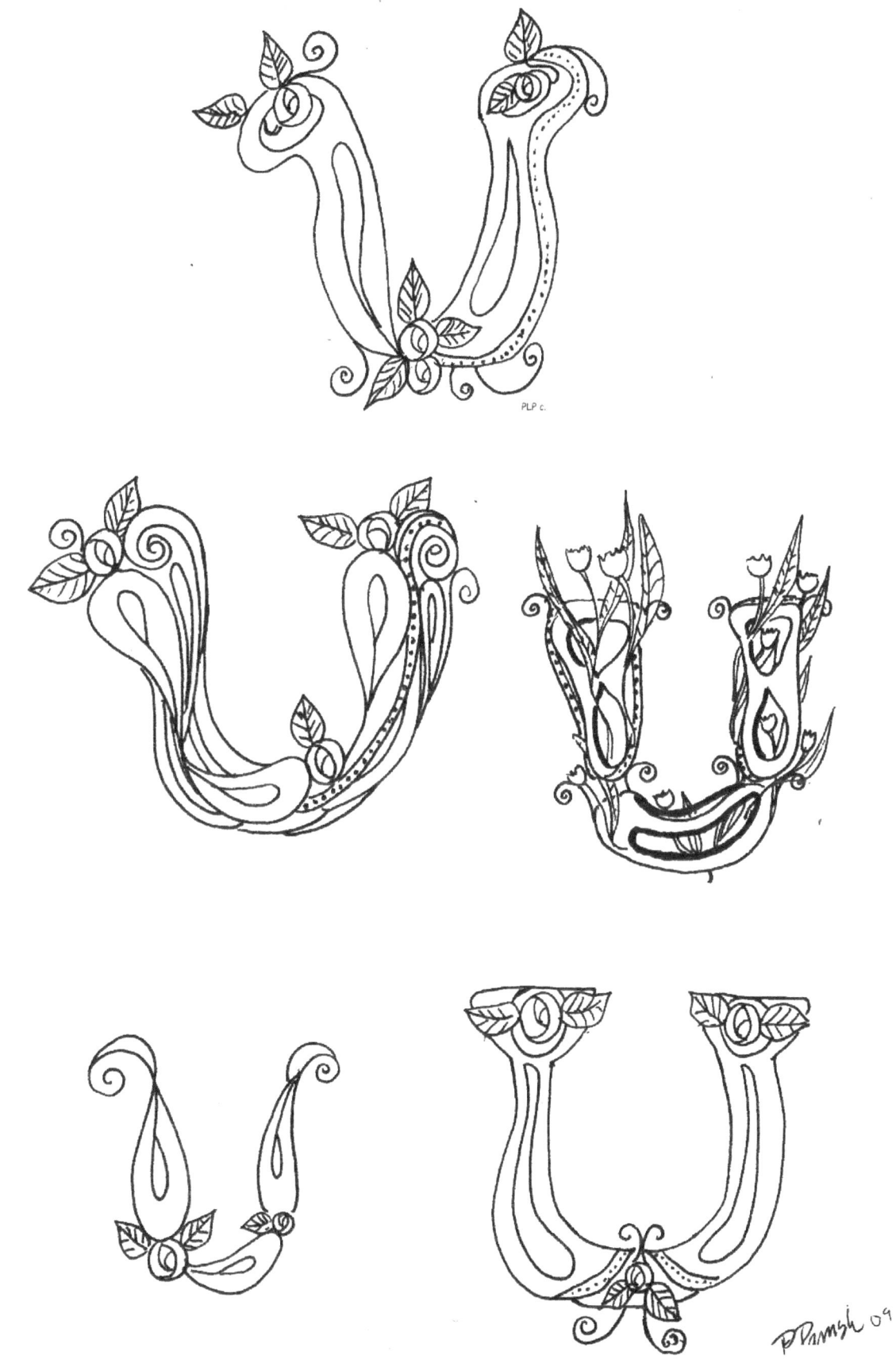

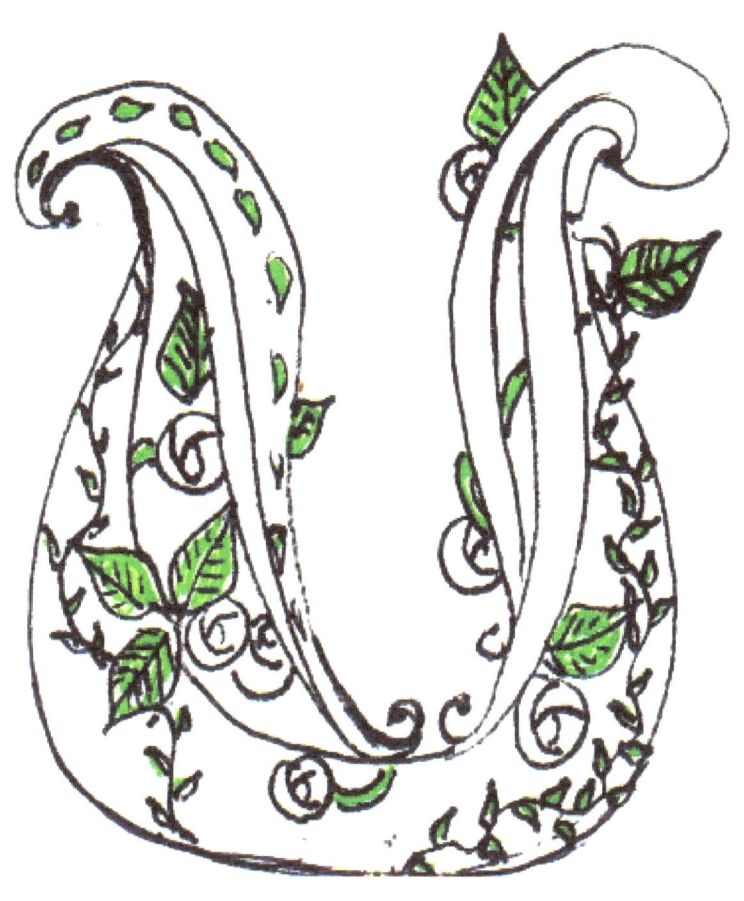

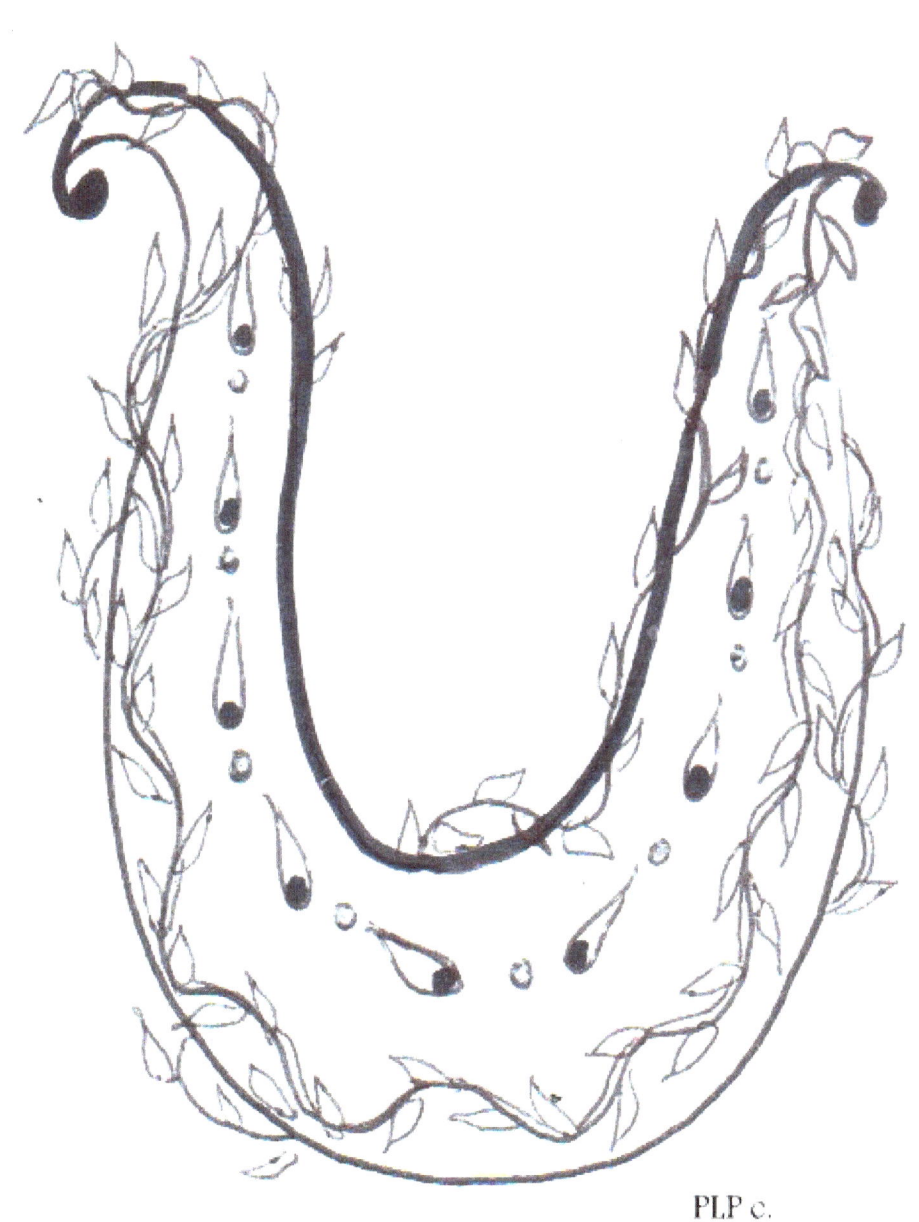

PLP c.

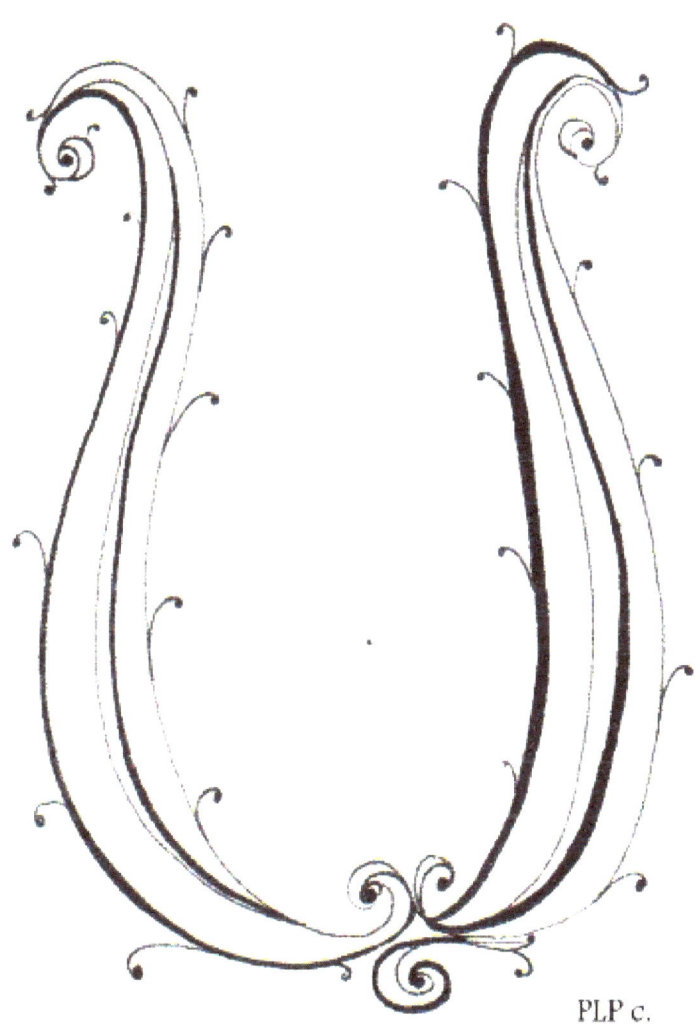

PLP c.

I hope the letter U's in your life will be more amazing than ever!

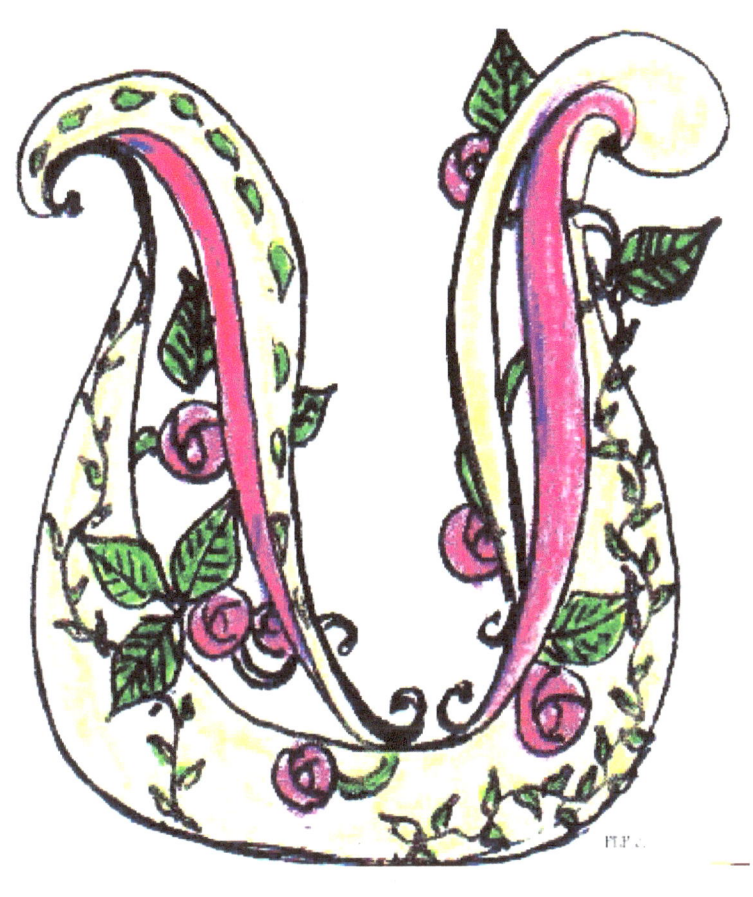

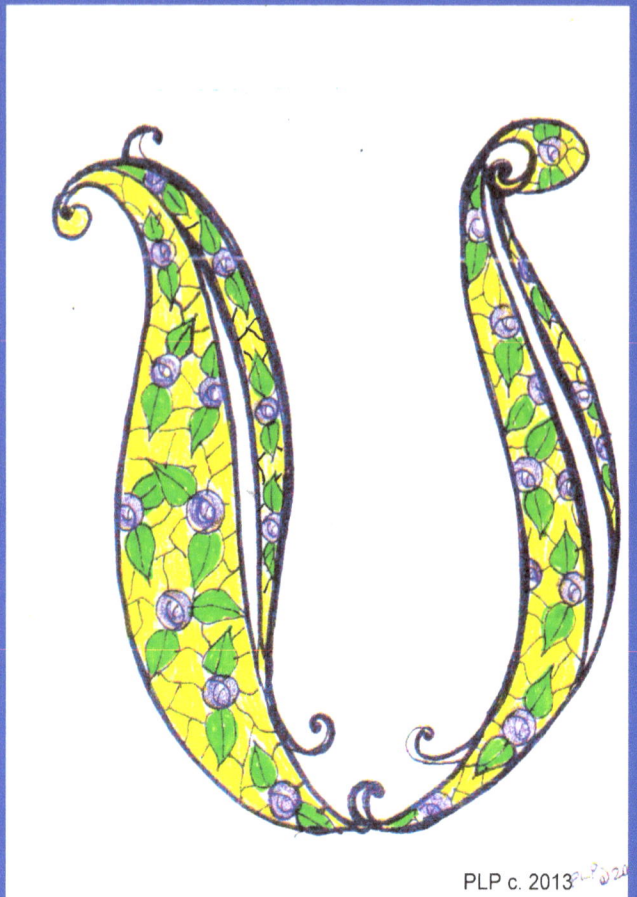

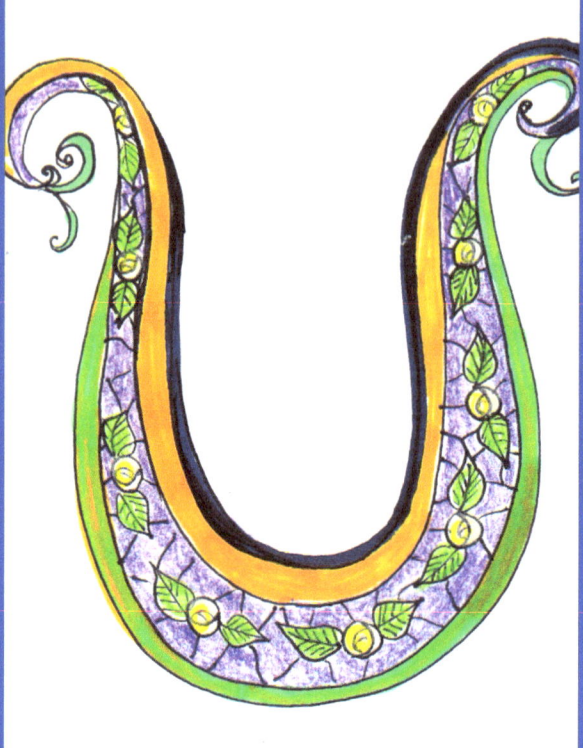

PLP c. 2013

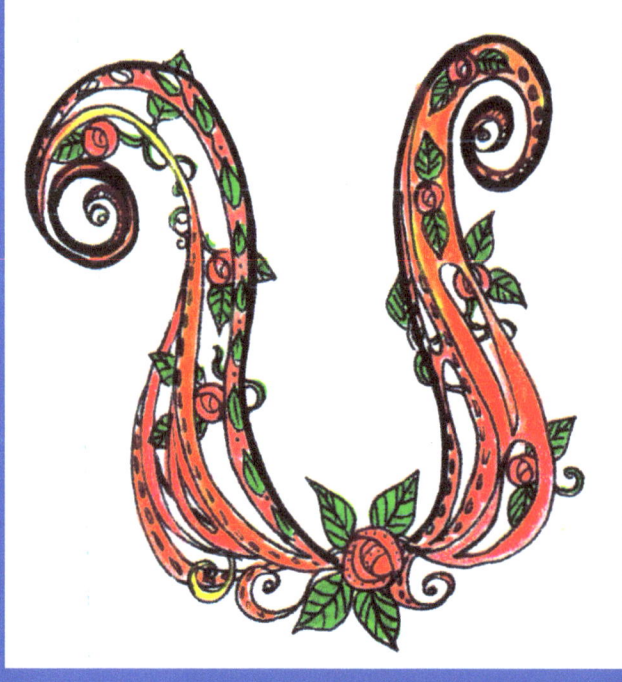

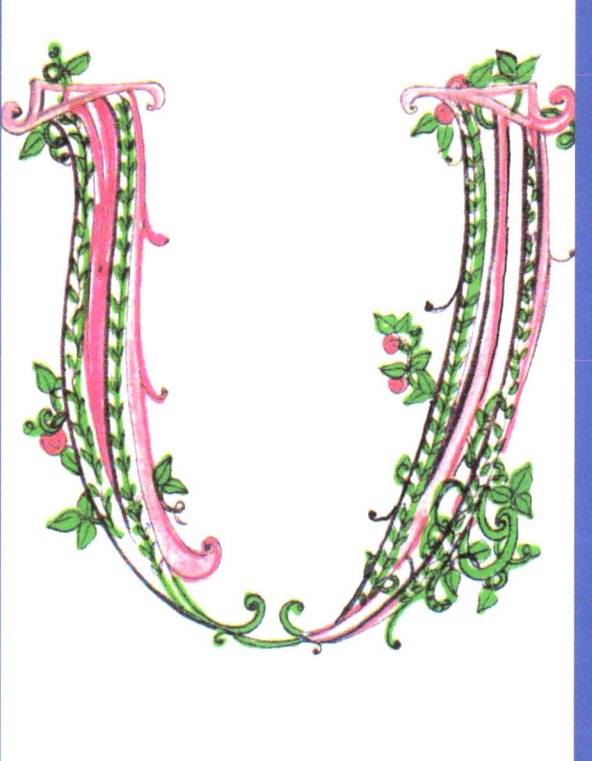

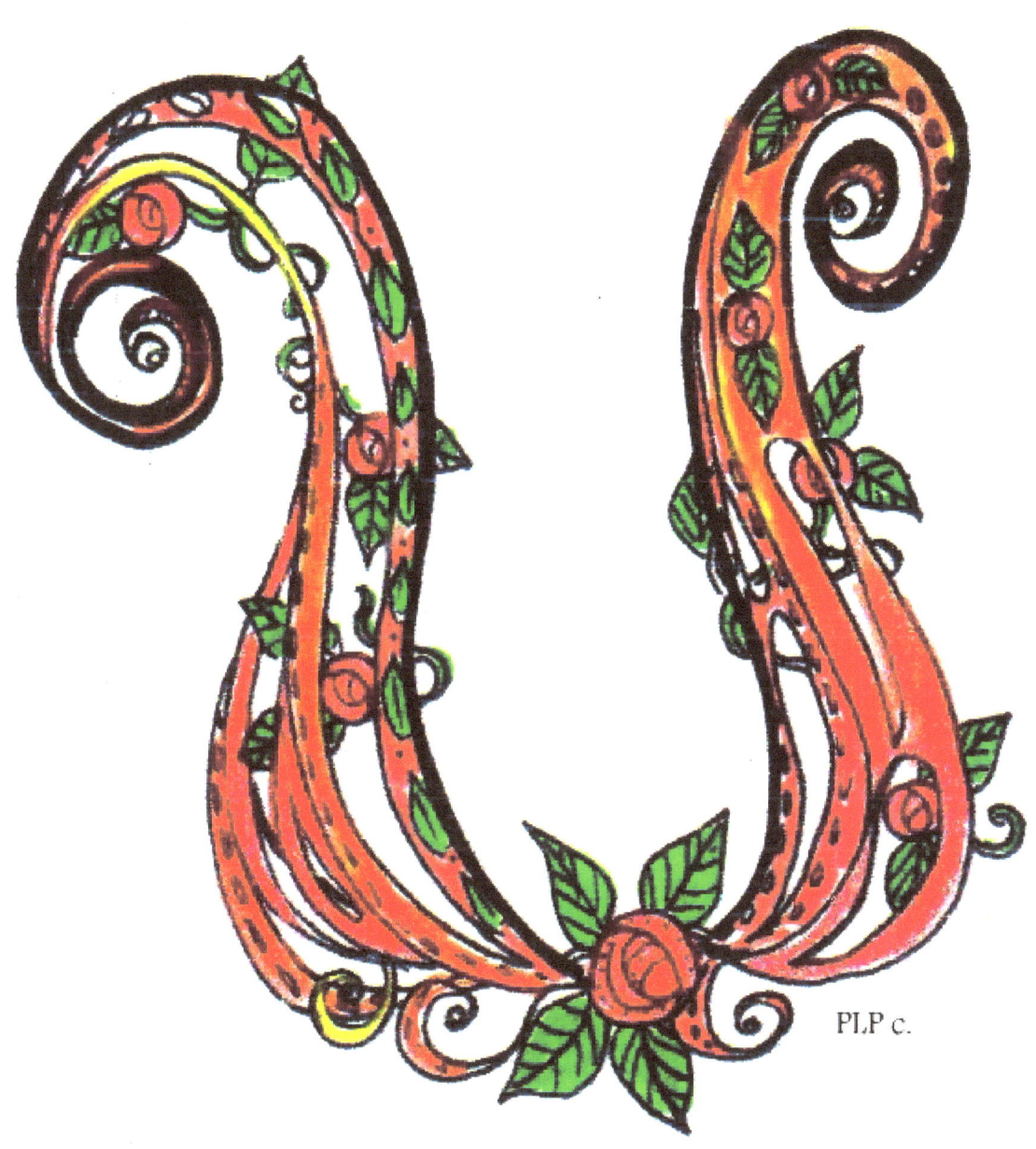

PLP c.

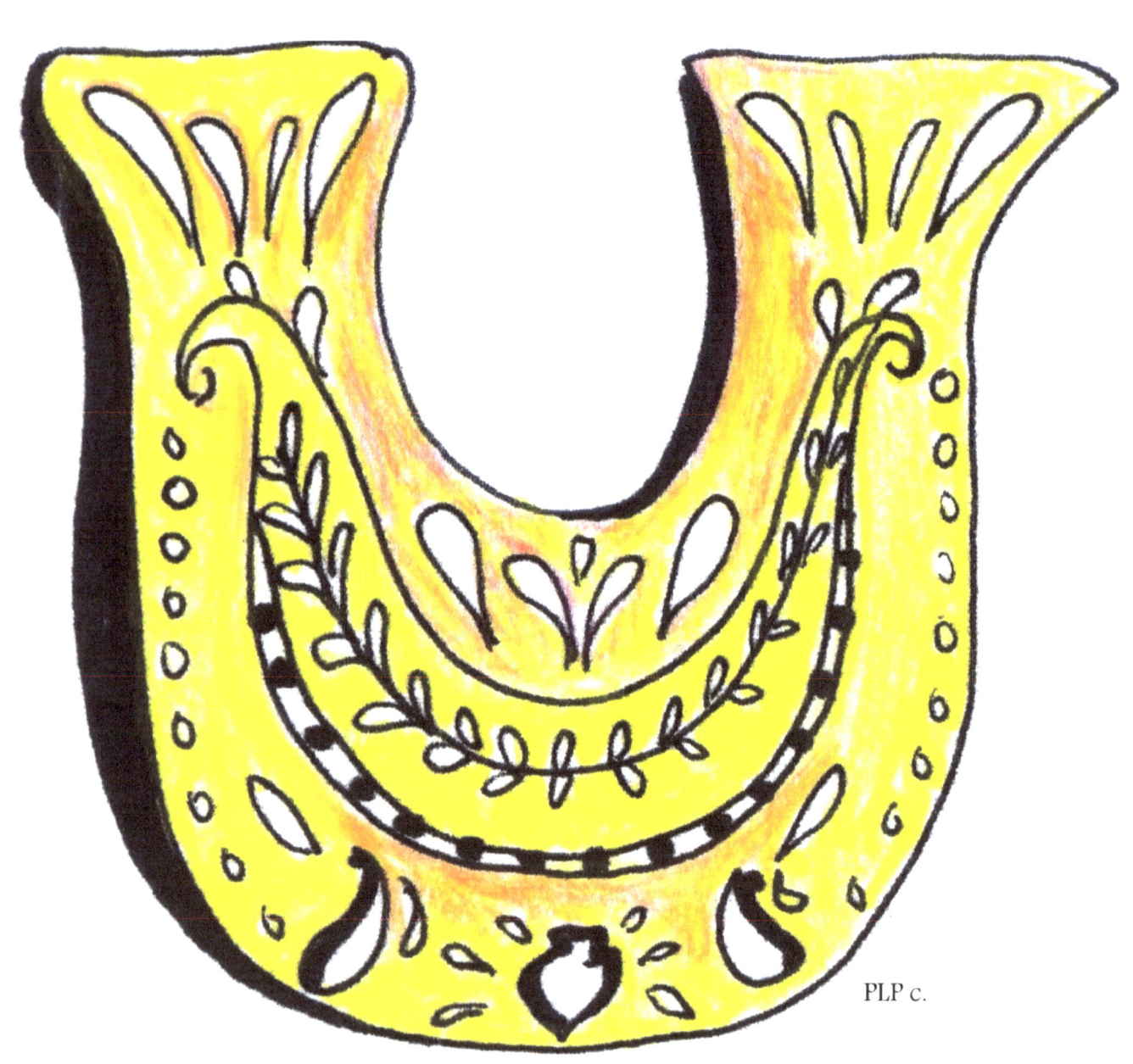

PLP c.

You may cut out and use these letters as a unique

sign somewhere in your life.   How UNIQUE.

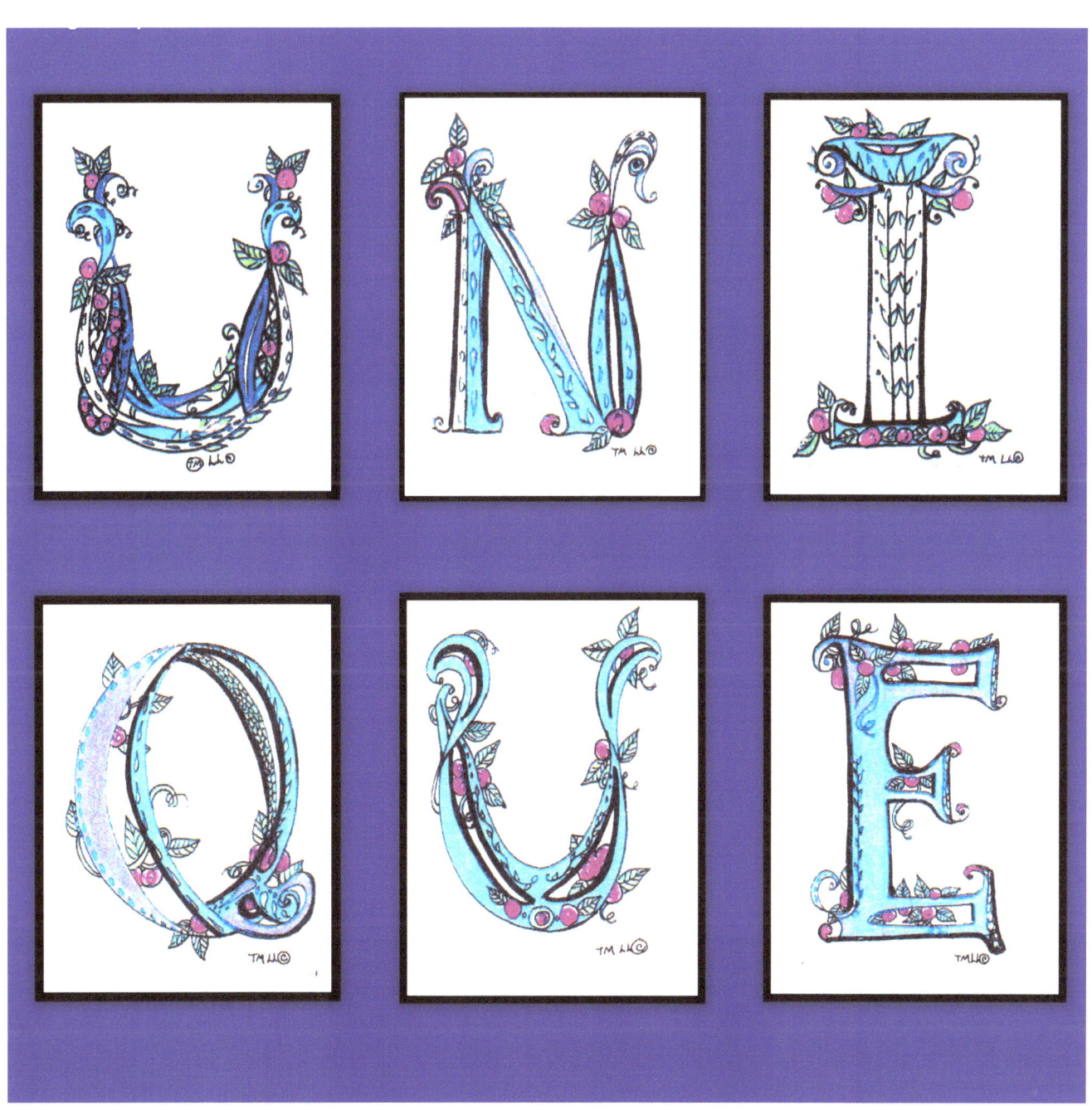